A long time ago, when the world was new, all the trees kept their leaves during the wintertime. The leaves helped the trees stay warm. But one winter, that all changed.

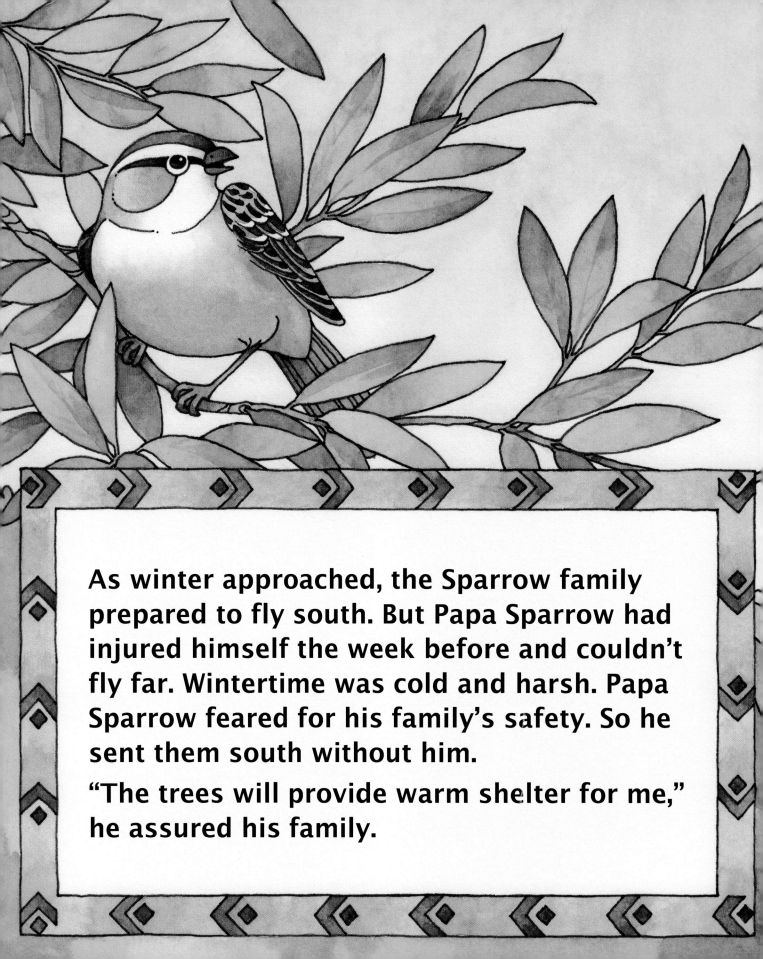

As winter approached, the Sparrow family prepared to fly south. But Papa Sparrow had injured himself the week before and couldn't fly far. Wintertime was cold and harsh. Papa Sparrow feared for his family's safety. So he sent them south without him.

"The trees will provide warm shelter for me," he assured his family.

The rest of the Sparrow family headed south. Papa Sparrow fluttered over to Maple. "Hello, Maple. Can you help me, please?" whispered Papa Sparrow.

"Help you? With what?" replied Maple.

"My wing is hurt and I could not fly south with my family. Can I take shelter in your beautiful, bushy leaves for the winter?" asked Papa Sparrow.

Maple drew her leaves in tight. "I do not know you. And I like to sleep during the cold, winter days. Birds are always singing and chirping and making lots of noise," said Maple. "You may not stay for the winter in my beautiful, bushy leaves."

Papa Sparrow was deeply saddened by Maple's words. He hung his head and fluttered away. *Oak is old and wise, maybe he will let me stay with him for the winter,* thought Papa Sparrow.

"Hello, Oak. Can you help me, please?" whispered Papa Sparrow.

"Help you? With what?" replied Oak.

"My wing is hurt and I could not fly south with my family. Can I take shelter in your big, strong branches for the winter?" asked Papa Sparrow.

"*Grrr.*" Oak growled. "I do not know you. And how do I know you won't eat all of my acorns? Birds are always looking for food," said Oak. "You may not stay for the winter in my big, strong branches."

Papa Sparrow was deeply saddened by Oak's words. He hung his head and fluttered away. *Willow is gentle and kind, maybe she will let me stay with her for the winter,* thought Papa Sparrow.

"Hello, Willow. Can you help me, please?" whispered Papa Sparrow.

"Help you? With what?" replied Willow.

"My wing is hurt and I could not fly south with my family. Can I take shelter in your gentle, hanging foliage for the winter?" asked Papa Sparrow.

"Oh, my," Willow gasped. "I do not know you. And how do I know you won't damage my lovely, gorgeous leaves? Birds are always flying and pecking and moving," said Willow. "You may not stay for the winter in my gentle, hanging foliage."

Papa Sparrow was deeply saddened by Willow's words. He hung his head and fluttered away. Papa Sparrow had asked every one of the strong, bushy, beautiful trees of the forest if he could take shelter with them for the winter. And they had all turned him away. *Spruce is prickly and has lots of needles, and he doesn't look as warm as Maple, Oak, or Willow, but maybe he will let me stay with him for the winter,* thought Papa Sparrow.

"Hello, Spruce. Can you help me, please?" whispered Papa Sparrow.

"Help you? With what?" replied Spruce.

"My wing is hurt and I could not fly south with my family. Can I take shelter in your needles for the winter?" asked Papa Sparrow.

"Tiny Sparrow, my needles are small and not very warm and I don't have as many branches as the other trees. But you are welcome to stay the winter with me. I will try to keep you warm," said Spruce. "And I am sure my friends, Pine and Juniper, will help as well."

"Hello, Sparrow, I am Pine. I am tall and slim, but I will do my best to block the wind from you and Spruce," said Pine.

"Hello, Sparrow, I am Juniper. I have some yummy berries that I will share with you," said Juniper.

Papa Sparrow hopped with joy. "Thank you, Spruce, Pine, and Juniper, for being so helpful to me. When my family returns, I will tell them of your kindness."

That night, Winter Wind rustled through the forest with great force. Her winds were cold and harsh. Every leaf that she touched fell to the ground.

When morning arrived, all of the forest trees were left with no leaves, except for Spruce and Pine and Juniper.

"Why do they still have their prickly, little needles?" questioned Maple.

"And look, Juniper still has all of his berries," bellowed Oak. "All of my acorns are on the ground."

"I demand an explanation!" cried Willow.

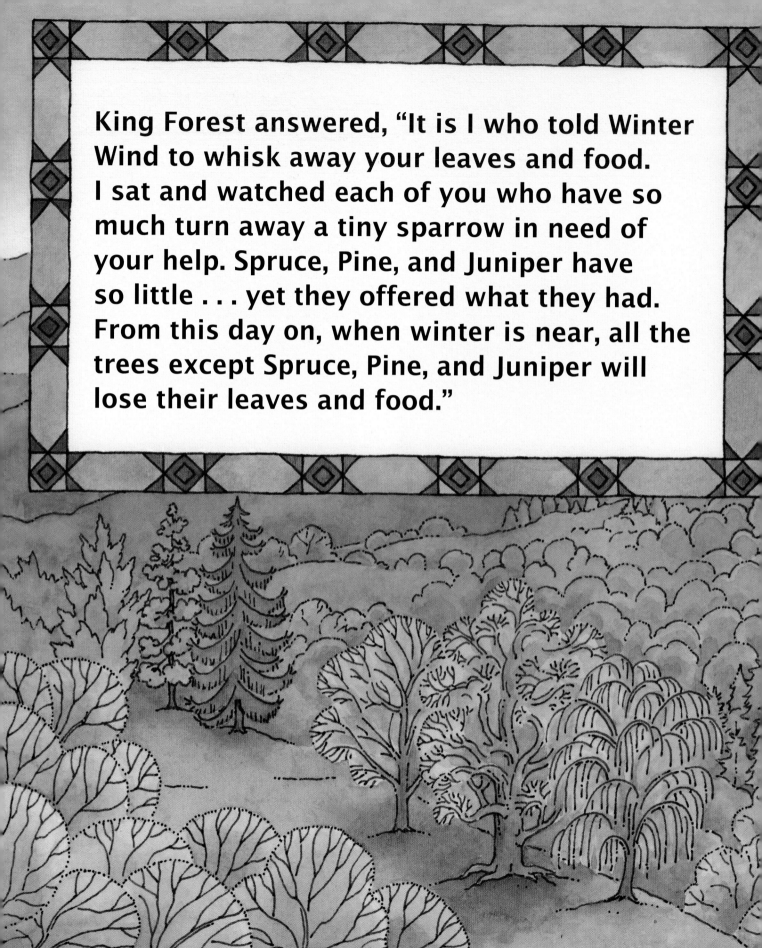

King Forest answered, "It is I who told Winter Wind to whisk away your leaves and food. I sat and watched each of you who have so much turn away a tiny sparrow in need of your help. Spruce, Pine, and Juniper have so little . . . yet they offered what they had. From this day on, when winter is near, all the trees except Spruce, Pine, and Juniper will lose their leaves and food."

And to this day, when autumn arrives, the selfish trees' leaves wither and fall to the ground. They no longer keep the trees warm through the cold, harsh winter months.

For Creative Minds

Chipping Sparrow Migration

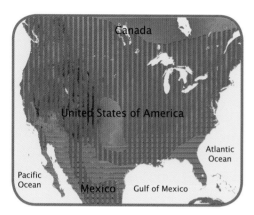

Chipping sparrows live in North America. Their summer breeding grounds cover most of the United States and parts of Canada and Mexico. In the fall, chipping sparrows travel (migrate) to the southern United States and Mexico. They travel in flocks with other migrating birds, especially other sparrow species.

There are a few places in the continental US where chipping sparrows do not live. But even in these areas, they can be seen during their migration.

Bird Watching Tips: Chipping Sparrow

Chipping sparrows have rust-orange feathers on the tops of their heads and a black line across their eyes. These colors are brightest during the summer breeding season and fade at other times of the year.

Can you spot any chipping sparrows? Use these tips to look for signs of chipping sparrows in your area.

- In the fall and winter, chipping sparrows often search for food (forage) in groups. Watch for flocks on the ground near trees.

- Listen for a long, loud trill or small *chip* sounds.

- Chipping sparrows like to live in parks, neighborhoods, pine forests, and open woodlands.

- Female chipping sparrows build nests 3-10 feet (1-3 meters) off the ground. Their nests are usually in evergreen trees, but sometimes in deciduous trees. Most nests take about 3 to 4 days to build. Chipping sparrow nests are loose cups of roots, grasses, and animal hair hidden in the leaves at the end of a branch. After finishing the nest, the female lays 2-7 sky blue eggs with a few dark blotches.

The Birds and the Trees

A **habitat** is a place where a plant or animal lives and grows. All living things work in their habitat to meet their **basic needs**: food, water, air and shelter. After meeting their basic needs, living things need to make new living things like themselves (reproduce). Living things also need to protect themselves from harm.

Plants and animals have to share their habitat. Birds and trees help each other in different ways. They can help each other meet their basic needs, reproduce, or protect themselves.

Read the sentences below and decide whether the action helps the birds or the trees.

1. Birds eat seeds, flowers, and berries that grow on trees.
2. Birds carry a tree's seeds to different places so they can grow into new trees.
3   Tree branches provide a place for birds to build their nests.
4. Birds protect trees by eating insects that could harm the trees.
5. Trees shelter birds from the weather.
6. Trees have nooks and holes where birds can hide food to eat later.

Helps birds: 1, 3, 5, 6
Helps trees: 2, 4

Tree Adaptations

All living things need energy to live and grow. Some animals eat other animals for food (carnivores). Other animals eat plants for food (herbivores). But plants don't eat animals or other plants. Plants make their own sugary food, through a process called **photosynthesis**. Plants need three things to make their food: energy from the sun, water, and carbon dioxide.

Plant leaves absorb energy from sunlight. Plants have roots that take in water from the ground. Carbon dioxide is a gas in the air. Leaves have small openings that let in carbon dioxide. But these openings can also let water out. Different types of trees have different adaptations so they don't lose too much water through their leaves.

Trees that drop their leaves are called **deciduous** trees. Deciduous trees generally have broad, flat leaves. These leaves can absorb lots of carbon dioxide and energy from the sun. But they also let more water evaporate into the air. In the winter, the weather is often cold and dry. When the air is dry, plants lose more water through their leaves. Deciduous trees drop their leaves in the fall to protect against water-loss. When the spring rains come, they grow new leaves for the year.

Trees that keep their leaves all year round are called **evergreen** trees. Evergreens usually have small, needle-like leaves. Because the leaves are so small and narrow, the tree needs lots of needles to gather enough carbon dioxide and energy from the sun. These leaves have a thick, waxy coat. This coat protects the leaves against water-loss. Evergreen trees keep their leaves through the cold, dry winter.

Evergreen or Deciduous

Use clues from the story to sort the trees below into evergreen trees or deciduous trees. Answers are below.

juniper   oak   maple

pine   willow   spruce

Evergreen: juniper, pine, spruce
Deciduous: oak, maple, willow

This is an adaptation of a Native American folktale. Earliest sources, dating back to the beginning of the 20th century, do not name the story's culture of origin. Modern sources commonly attribute the story to the Cherokee. However, through our rigorous vetting process, we have confirmed with storytellers, historians, and cultural specialists from both the Eastern Band of Cherokee Indians and the Cherokee Nation that they are unaware of this story or its origins.

Folktales are part of how people express their own culture. They also provide a way for people to learn about the history and values of cultures different from their own. When a story becomes separated from its culture, this opportunity is lost on both sides.

To my wonderful husband, Ricky, who always provides me with an endless supply of warmth, kindness, and love.—SC
For Herman, with love.—SD
Thanks to Peter McGowan of the US Fish and Wildlife Service for reviewing the accuracy of the information in this book.

Library of Congress Cataloging-in-Publication Data

Chriscoe, Sharon, 1973-
  The sparrow and the trees / by Sharon Chriscoe ; illustrated by Susan Detwiler.
    pages cm
  ISBN 978-1-62855-633-9 (English hardcover) -- ISBN 978-1-62855-638-4 (English pbk.) -- ISBN 978-1-62855-648-3 (English downloadable ebook) -- ISBN 978-1-62855-658-2 (English interactive dual-language ebook) -- ISBN 978-1-62855-643-8 (Spanish pbk.) -- ISBN 978-1-62855-653-7 (Spanish downloadable ebook) -- ISBN 978-1-62855-663-6 (Spanish interactive dual-language ebook) 1. Cherokee Indians--Folklore. 2. Trees--Folklore. 3. Sparrows--Folklore. 4. Kindness--Folklore. I. Detwiler, Susan, illustrator. II. Title.
  E99.C5C655 2015
  398.2089'97557--dc23
                              2015009046

Translated into Spanish: *El gorrión y los árboles*

Lexile® Level: AD 680L
key phrases for educators: plant adaptations, basic needs, character, seasons

Bibliography:
Alles, Hemesh. "Plants." *World Book's Young Scientist, Vol. 5: Living World. Plants.* Chicago: World Book, 1992. 64-117. Print.
"Birds' Role in Ecosystems." *Science Learning.* 27 June 2011. Web. 14 Mar. 2015.
"Chipping Sparrow: Life History" *All About Birds.* n.d. Web. 13 Mar. 2015.
Dorros, Arthur, and S. D. Schindler. *A Tree Is Growing.* New York: Scholastic, 1997. Print.
Hester, Nigel S., Angela Owen, and Ron Haywood. *The Living Tree.* New York: F. Watts, 1990. Print.
Holbrook, Florence. *The Book of Nature Myths.* Cambridge: The Riverside Press, 1902. *Sacred-Texts.* Web. March 10, 2015.
Johnson, Rebecca L., and Phyllis V. Saroff. *A Walk in the Deciduous Forest.* Minneapolis: Carolrhoda, 2001. Print.
Latimer, Jonathan P., Karen Stray. Nolting, and Roger Tory Peterson. *Backyard Birds.* Boston: Houghton Mifflin, 1999. Print.
"Learn About Trees & Forests." *Home Science Tools.* n.d. Web. 01 Mar. 2015.
Perkins, Sid. "Fall is leaving." *Missourian's Mini-MO newspaper for kids* 7 Oct. 1996: 4. *National Association of Science Writers.* Web. 11 Mar. 2015.
Peterson, Roger Tory, and Virginia Marie Peterson. *A Field Guide to the Birds: a Completely New Guide to All the Birds of Eastern and Central North America.* Boston: Houghton Mifflin, 1980. M370. Print.
Pine, Jonathan, and Ken Joudrey. *Trees.* New York, NY: HarperCollins, 1995. Print.

Manufactured in China, June 2015
This product conforms to CPSIA 2008
First Printing

Text Copyright 2015 © by Sharon Chriscoe
Illustration Copyright 2015 © by Susan Detwiler

Arbordale Publishing
Mt. Pleasant, SC 29464
www.ArbordalePublishing.com